# The Life and World of

# JULIUS CAESAR

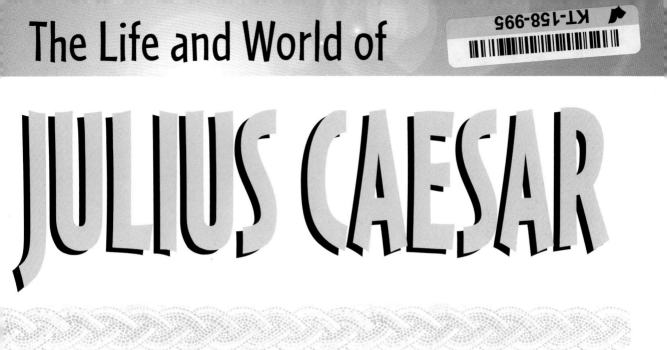

## Struan Reid

Heinemann
LIBRARY

**H** www.heinemann.co.uk/library
Visit our website to find out more information about Heinemann Library books.

To order:
☎ Phone 44 (0) 1865 888066
▤ Send a fax to 44 (0) 1865 314091
▭ Visit the Heinemann Library Bookshop at www.heinemann.co.uk/library to browse our catalogue and order online.

First published in Great Britain by Heinemann Library,
Halley Court, Jordan Hill, Oxford OX2 8EJ
a division of Reed Educational and Professional Publishing Ltd.
Heinemann is a registered trademark of Reed Educational & Professional Publishing Ltd.

OXFORD  MELBOURNE  AUCKLAND
JOHANNESBURG  BLANTYRE  GABORONE
IBADAN  PORTSMOUTH (NH)  USA  CHICAGO

Designed by Celia Floyd
Illustrated by Jeff Edwards and Joanna Brooker
Originated by Ambassador Litho Ltd
Printed by Wing King Tong in Hong Kong.

ISBN 0 431 14775 2
06 05 04 03 02
10 9 8 7 6 5 4 3 2 1

**British Library Cataloguing in Publication Data**

Reid, Struan
  The life and world of Julius Caesar
  1. Caesar, Julius, 100 B.C. – 44  B.C.
  2. Heads of state – Rome - Biography - Juvenile literature 3.Rome - History - Republic, 265–30 B.C. – Juvenile literature
  I. Title   II. Julius Caesar
  937'.05'092

**Acknowledgements**

The Publishers would like to thank the following for permission to reproduce photographs: AKG: pp9, 26, 29; Ancient Art and Architecture: pp6, 14, 18, 19, 22, 23; The Art Archive: pp13, 16, 17, 20, 25, 27; British Museum: pp10, 15; Trevor Clifford: p8; Corbis: p11; Montreal Museum of Fine Arts: p21; Scala: pp4, 7, 12, 24, 28.

Cover photograph reproduced with permission of Scala.

Our thanks to Rebecca Vickers for her help in the preparation of this book.

Every effort has been made to contact copyright holders of any material reproduced in this book. Any omissions will be rectified in subsequent printings if notice is given to the Publisher.

# Contents

Who was Julius Caesar?     4

Caesar's early life     6

Growing up in Rome     8

A Greek adventure     10

Growing power     12

Climbing up     14

Caesar and the Triumvirate     16

Caesar the great general     18

Who will rule?     20

Crossing the Rubicon     22

Caesar the dictator     24

One demand too many     26

After Julius Caesar     28

Glossary     30

Timeline     31

Further reading & websites     31

Places to visit     31

Index     32

Any words appearing in the text in bold, **like this**, are explained in the glossary.

# Who was Julius Caesar?

Julius Caesar was a Roman **politician** and general who lived more than 2000 years ago. He was perhaps one of the most **ambitious** men who has ever lived. He would let nothing and no one get in the way of his climb to power.

## Rome in Caesar's time

In the time of Julius Caesar, Rome was one of the most powerful states in the western world. It had been governed as a **republic** with elected rulers for 400 years. Caesar tricked, bribed and bullied his way to the top, and by the time of his death he held the most powerful position that the Roman Republic had ever seen. He introduced many changes to the way Rome and its **empire** were ruled. These were to remain in place for the next 500 years. As a result of Caesar's work, Rome ruled over an empire that was the largest and most powerful the world had ever seen.

## Stabbed to death

Caesar's ambitions eventually became too much for the other political families of Rome, and he was stabbed to death by a group of politicians. By then the days of the Republic were already numbered. Julius Caesar had made so many changes to the government that it could never return to the way it had been run. His work was continued by his adopted son, Octavian, who eventually became the first Roman **emperor**.

▼ Julius Caesar rose to become the most powerful man in Rome and changed the course of world history forever.

## How do we know?

We know about Julius Caesar and about ancient Roman **civilization** from the writings and records the Romans kept. Very few original Roman books and papers have survived, but we do have later copies made by **monks** and **scholars**. These include works of history, **politics** and **philosophy**, as well as plays, poems and letters. Other information comes from stone **inscriptions** and Roman coins.

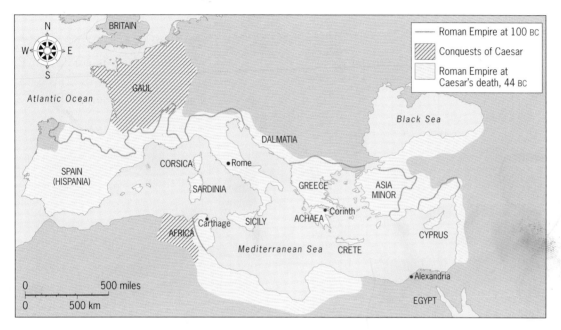

▲ This map shows the extent of the Roman Empire at the time of Julius Caesar's birth in about 100 BC, and at his death in 44 BC. During that time the empire expanded far beyond the shores of the Mediterranean Sea.

## Key dates

| | |
|---|---|
| About 100 BC | Birth of Julius Caesar |
| 63 BC | Caesar is made Chief Priest of Rome |
| 58–50 BC | Caesar's **campaigns** in Gaul |
| 55–54 BC | Caesar's invasions of Britain |
| 45 BC | Caesar becomes **dictator** for life, and ruler of the Roman world |
| 44 BC | Death of Julius Caesar |

## Watch the date

The letters 'BC' after a year date mean before the birth of Jesus Christ. Years before Christ are counted backwards towards zero.

# Caesar's early life

Gaius Julius Caesar was born about the twelfth day of Quinctilis (later renamed the month of July after him) in about 100 BC. His father, also named Gaius Julius Caesar, was a government official called a **praetor**. His mother, Aurelia, came from an old and powerful noble family. His father's family, known as the Julii, was also very ancient and claimed to be descended from the goddess Venus.

Caesar's parents were not very rich, and the boy grew up with a strict, plain family life. They lived in the city of Rome and their house was comfortably but simply furnished. There were some household servants, such as maids, cooks and **slaves**, and Aurelia had a nursemaid to help her raise her son and his two younger sisters.

▲ This wall painting from a house in the town of Pompeii, shows what the inside of a Roman house would have looked like.

## Schooldays

Like the sons of most noble families, from a young age Caesar was educated by a private **tutor**. When he was about eleven years old he was probably sent to a secondary school, called a *grammaticus*, where he studied subjects such as history, **philosophy**, geography, mathematics, **astronomy** and music. He was also taught the Greek language by a man called Antonius Gnipho.

Greek was one of the most important subjects at school. Greek **culture** had a very strong influence on the Romans, as they had inherited their religion and much of their way of life from the Greeks. Works of Greek and Roman literature were studied in great detail, and students were expected to learn whole passages off by heart.

▶ Young men who wanted to become politicians needed to master the art of **oratory**, or public speaking. They were taught how to write speeches properly and how to present them well.

## Preparing for public service

As Julius Caesar was born into a **patrician** family, he was expected to have a career in **politics** or the army. To do this, he had to learn to speak in public. From the age of about thirteen he was sent to a teacher of public speaking, called a *rhetor*.

# Growing up in Rome

In 85 BC, when Caesar was fifteen years old, his father died. As the new head of the family, the young man was left to look after his mother and two younger sisters. The following year, Caesar officially became an adult at a ceremony attended by lots of other young men from noble families. The young Julius Caesar is described at this time as 'tall, fair and well-built'. He had a broad face and dark, piercing eyes.

## A useful marriage

It was normal for Roman parents to choose husbands and wives for their children. While he was still a boy, Caesar's father had chosen a future bride for him, called Cossutia. When his father died, Caesar broke off the engagement. Instead he married a woman called Cornelia. She was the daughter of Cinna – one of the most powerful men in Rome. Their wedding was about 85 BC and their daughter, Julia, was born about a year later.

▲ The Forum was a large square in the centre of Rome which contained many of the city's most important buildings. It was here that Caesar officially became an adult. These ruins are all that is left today.

## Forced into hiding

With his powerful new family connections, Caesar began to climb up the ladder to power. He became an officer in the army and he also held a junior position in the government. But in 82 BC, when he was about eighteen, Caesar's world was shattered.

In that year a **politician** called Sulla came to power. Sulla viewed Caesar as a threat to his authority and tried to have the young man murdered. Caesar was forced to go into hiding in the hills outside Rome.

▶ Lucius Cornelius Sulla was the leader of one of the Roman political parties. His ideas were opposed to those which Caesar's family supported.

### The Roman Republic

Rome was a **republic**, which meant that its rulers were elected by the **citizens**. The most important citizens, called the **patricians**, belonged to the old noble families. Only patricians were allowed to become members of the **Senate**, which was the group of people who decided how Rome was governed.

# A Greek adventure

After some months in hiding, Caesar was pardoned by Sulla and allowed to return to Rome. Even so, he decided that it would be wise to stay away. In 80 BC, he served as a soldier in Greece under the command of a general called Minucius Thermus. Caesar was awarded an important military decoration, called the *corona civica*, for his part in the capture of the city of Mitylene on the island of Lesbos.

## A skilful speaker

In 78 BC Sulla died. It was safe for Caesar to return to Rome. He earned a reputation as a skilled **orator** when he acted as a lawyer at the trial of an old friend of Sulla's. Although Caesar did not win the case, his performance made him famous.

## Captured by pirates

In 76 BC, when he was about 24, Caesar decided to travel to the Greek island of Rhodes to study under a famous **philosopher**, called Apollonius Molon. On the way, his ship was captured by **pirates** and Caesar was taken to the island of Pharmacusa (modern Farmakonission).

▶ A Roman soldier wore a metal helmet, an armoured tunic and leg guards, and carried a shield. He fought with a spear, sword and dagger.

The pirates demanded a **ransom** of 20 gold **talents**, which was a huge sum of money. Caesar told them he was worth at least 50 talents! He also told them that as soon as he was released he would be back to kill them. After six weeks, the ransom was paid and Caesar was set free. He immediately sailed back to Pharmacusa. True to his word, he had all the pirates executed.

▲ Caesar was travelling to the Greek island of Rhodes, just off the western coast of Turkey, when he was attacked by pirates.

### Pirate attack

Pirates were a terrible menace to ships in the Mediterranean Sea. Although the Romans ruled many of the lands round the Mediterranean, they did not control the sea itself and their ships were often attacked by pirates. The Romans did not manage to stamp out piracy for many years.

# Growing power

The story of Caesar's capture by the **pirates** ensured that his name now became even more famous back in Rome. This was very important for a man who had **political ambitions**. The more publicity he received, the better. The **citizens** of Rome were beginning to regard Caesar as a very strong leader.

## *The push for power*

Caesar returned to Rome in 73 BC and now, aged about 27, he began his real push for power. He used his family connections to open as many doors as he could. He was appointed a Priest of Jupiter and this position introduced him to many important people. In 69 BC he was elected to the post of military **tribune**. Although this was not a very important job, it was a useful step up the ladder to power.

In 68 BC, Caesar was elected to the junior post of *Quaestor* for one year and sent to work in Spain. This was a very remote posting. Maybe other **politicians** were growing alarmed at Caesar's lust for power and wanted to get him out of the way.

▶ As a Priest of Jupiter, Caesar would have been expected to take part in ceremonies at a temple like this, the Temple of Fortuna Virilis in Rome.

## A new wife

Before he left Rome, Caesar's wife Cornelia had died from an illness. On his return the next year he married again. His new wife, Pompeia, was the cousin of a famous general, called Gnaeus Pompeius Magnus (usually known as Pompey), and the granddaughter of Caesar's old enemy, Sulla. She was also extremely rich, which would be very useful in helping her new husband buy his way into power.

▶ This is a bust of Alexander the Great (356–323 BC), King of Macedon and conqueror of half the known world. He died at the age of only 33. Caesar admired Alexander and wanted to imitate him.

### The face of greatness

While Caesar was in Spain, he is said to have visited Cadiz, where he saw a statue of Alexander the Great. Caesar is meant to have sighed and said that by the time Alexander was his age he had achieved so much, but he himself had still not done anything of any real importance.

# Climbing up

Caesar could be very charming, and after he had returned to Rome from Spain he set out to make friends in high places. One of these was a **senator** called Marcus Licinius Crassus, the richest man in Rome.

### A new job

With the backing of his powerful new friends, Caesar was made *Curule Aedile* in 65 BC. This was a very important post. It placed him in charge of the upkeep of all the public buildings in Rome, and also the organization of public entertainment. If he played his cards right, Caesar was now in the best position to win a lot of popularity and support from the people of Rome.

He asked his new friend Crassus to help him. With Crassus's money Caesar was able to pay for huge public entertainments, organizing spectacular **gladiator** fights and magnificent religious festivals for the people of Rome. The city had never seen such wonderful displays. Many senators said that they were too expensive, but the people loved them.

▶ This terracotta statue shows two gladiators in action. The fight normally continued to the death, but a defeated gladiator could appeal for mercy.

### Chief Priest of Rome

Caesar's **political** career really took off in 63 BC, when he was appointed *Pontifex Maximus*, or Chief Priest of Rome. He was not a religious man, but he was not going to let that prevent him from gaining yet more power. This new post was absolutely perfect as a power-base from where he could plan his next move. Caesar was on the way up and nothing was going to stop him.

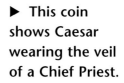

▶ This coin shows Caesar wearing the veil of a Chief Priest.

### Gladiator fights

Gladiators were prisoners, criminals, **slaves** or paid volunteers who fought for the public's entertainment. They fought against each other or against wild animals. While he was *Curule Aedile*, Caesar organized a show in which in one day alone 640 gladiators fought each other.

# Caesar and the Triumvirate

In July 63 BC, Caesar was elected to the important post of *praetor*. Two years later, he left Rome to become **governor** of the Roman **province** of Spain for a year. While he was there, he led a number of successful attacks on the local warriors. This added to his reputation back home and proved that he was a skilled military leader.

### Back to politics

Caesar returned to Rome in 60 BC and went back to his **political** work. The great Roman general Pompey had also returned after spectacular military victories in the **Middle East**. But Pompey had been so successful that the Roman **Senate** feared he was becoming too powerful. They decided not to give Pompey's soldiers the rewards of land that were customary after great victories. This was a huge insult to Pompey, who became very angry.

◀ This bronze statue of Caesar was probably made after he became a member of the Triumvirate in 60 BC, when he was one of the most important people in Rome.

Caesar decided that this was his chance. He struck a deal with Pompey and Crassus. They agreed to support his bid to become one of the two **consuls** for the year 59 BC. The post of consul was the most important political position in Rome. In return, Caesar promised to change certain laws to suit Pompey and Crassus. This agreement between the three men became known as the **Triumvirate**.

## Caesar becomes consul

Many officials were **bribed** by Crassus's money, and Caesar was soon elected one of the two consuls. He immediately gave Pompey's soldiers their land and introduced new tax laws that enabled Crassus to become even richer. The Triumvirate were now the most powerful men in Rome. No one dared challenge them.

▶ **This marble bust of Pompey shows him when he was a member of the Triumvirate.**

## Another wedding

In 62 BC, Caesar divorced his second wife, Pompeia. His third wife was Calpurnia, the daughter of a rich senator called Calpurnius Piso. At the same time Pompey married Caesar's daughter, Julia.

# Caesar the great general

**C**onsuls only served for a year, but when their term of office ended they were entitled to become **governor** of one of Rome's **provinces**. With all his bribes and lavish entertaining, Caesar was heavily in debt. He therefore needed to become governor of a very rich province. While he was still consul, he passed a law that meant he could become governor of not just one but three provinces: Cisalpine Gaul (now northern Italy), Transalpine Gaul (southern France) and Illyricum (Croatia).

## An opportunity in Gaul

This new job was an opportunity to make lots of money, and the chance for Caesar to show off his skills as a great military leader. This would be good publicity for him. A huge Roman army was stationed in Gaul. When Caesar arrived there, the first thing he did was to make sure that the soldiers were well looked after, with good pay and food. This made him very popular with the men. He knew that one day, quite soon, he would be relying on their support.

▼ The carving on this Roman sarcophagus (stone coffin) shows a battle between the Romans and Gauls.

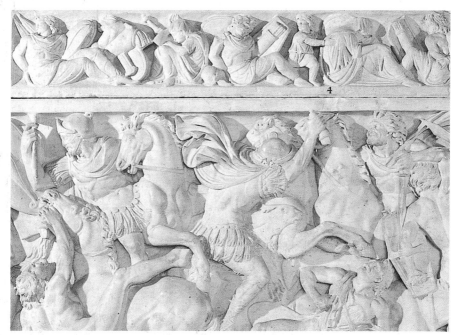

## Two expeditions to Britain

Beyond Gaul lay the island of Britain. In the years 55 BC and 54 BC Caesar launched two unsuccessful invasions of Britain. However, with his usual skill, Caesar managed to present these failures as successes which made him even more popular among the Roman people.

## Defeat of the Gauls

North of Transalpine Gaul, beyond the rule of Rome, lay the rich and fertile lands of northern France which were controlled by a number of **tribes**. In a **campaign** lasting two years, Caesar completely defeated these people and brought their lands under the direct rule of Rome. As always, he made sure that his victories were well reported back in Rome, so that everyone would know what a brilliant general he was.

▶ This statue is of Vercingetorix, leader of the Gauls of northern France. Julius Caesar finally defeated the Gauls in 51 BC.

# Who will rule?

While Caesar was away in Gaul, events in Rome were getting out of hand. Law and order was breaking down and it was impossible to hold elections.

The old ruling families resented the enormous power held by the **Triumvirate**. Some **senators** believed that if they could get Pompey on their side, they would be able to break the Triumvirate's control. They began to spread rumours that Caesar's military successes were so great that he was now growing too powerful. This made Pompey, who regarded himself as the greatest of all the generals, very jealous.

## *The death of Crassus*

As long as Crassus, the third member of the Triumvirate, remained in power the situation would not boil over. But in 53 BC he was killed in battle. More riots broke out in Rome and the **Senate** house was burnt down. Things were becoming so dangerous that the senators elected Pompey as **consul** to restore order. By now he was so jealous of Caesar's popularity that he turned against his old friend. On Pompey's orders, the Senate asked Caesar to return to Rome to face charges of **corruption**.

▶ Marcus Tullius Cicero was a senator who supported the old **republican** system of government and was a bitter enemy of Julius Caesar. He was brutally murdered in 43 BC.

## The battle lines are drawn

Caesar was now in a tricky position. If he agreed to return to Rome, he would probably be executed (killed). If he refused, he would be regarded as a criminal. He knew, however, that he had the support of his armies in Gaul. So the battle lines were now drawn for a **civil war** between his army and the Senate's army, led by Pompey.

▲ This 17th-century French painting by Jean Lemaire shows senators going to the Forum in Rome, where the main government buildings, including the Senate House, were built.

### Breaking ties

Pompey could have chosen Caesar as the second consul. But he wanted to destroy Caesar, so he chose instead a senator called Metellus Scipio. Caesar's daughter Julia, who had been married to Pompey, had died and Pompey now married Scipio's daughter. The ties that had linked Pompey and Caesar were broken.

# Crossing the Rubicon

In January 49 BC, Caesar and his army began to march towards Rome. They stopped when they reached the banks of the River Rubicon, the boundary that separated Gaul from Italy. Caesar knew that once he had crossed the river there would be no turning back. At this stage he is supposed to have said, 'The die is cast', meaning that he had to go on. He crossed into Italy and set out for Rome.

## *Pompey leaves Rome*

As Caesar marched south, many more soldiers flocked to join him. Hearing news of this approaching danger, many senators, including Pompey, fled to Greece where another Roman army loyal to the **Senate** was stationed. Caesar was able to enter Rome without a fight, and he spent several months there preparing for the showdown with Pompey.

▶ Caesar and his army would have sailed to Greece in ships like the one on this coin. A Roman warship was powered by oars, pulled by **slaves** below the decks.

## A battle in Greece

In 48 BC, Caesar and his army sailed to Greece in pursuit of Pompey. On 9 August the two armies finally came face to face at a place called the Plain of Pharsalus. Even though he had many more soldiers in his army, Pompey was defeated. He fled from the battlefield to Egypt, where he had more friends and supporters.

Caesar sailed to Egypt a few weeks later. When he arrived there, he was met by some Egyptian messengers who presented him with the head of Pompey. The great general had been murdered by his own men. His death made Caesar the undisputed leader of the Roman world.

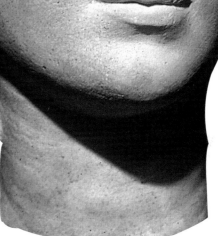

▶ Egypt was ruled by King Ptolemy XIII and his sister Cleopatra. Caeser was greatly impressed by Cleopatra's beauty and intelligence.

### Caesar and Cleopatra

Caesar helped Cleopatra to **depose** Ptolemy and become sole ruler of Egypt. Rumours soon spread that Caesar and Cleopatra were having a love affair. This was probably true, and when Caesar returned to Rome, Cleopatra went with him. After Caesar's death Cleopatra had another love affair with the Roman **politician** Mark Antony.

# Caesar the dictator

Caesar remained in Egypt for nearly a year. His enemies were regrouping, though, and waiting for a chance to attack. In 47 BC, Caesar defeated an Egyptian army led by Cleopatra's brother Ptolemy, then sailed to Spain where he defeated Pompey's remaining followers at the Battle of Munda. The **civil war** was at an end, and Caesar could return to Rome in triumph. He was now about 53 years old.

## *Dictator for life*

When he returned to Rome in 46 BC, Caesar held four different victory celebrations. He was also made **dictator** for life. The position of dictator was not new, but no one had been made dictator for life, and no dictator had ever been so powerful. Caesar stripped the **Senate** of its remaining powers, and in doing this dealt the final blow to the old noble families who had ruled the **republic** for so long.

▶ When a Roman general returned from a successful **campaign**, he was allowed to hold a victory parade through Rome, called a Triumph. This picture by Andrea Mantegna, painted between 1486–94, shows a scene from one of Caesar's Triumphs.

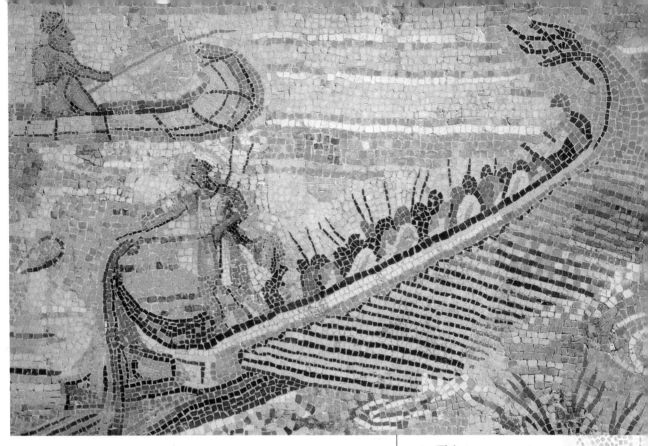

## Total power

Caesar may have acted illegally in grabbing all this power for himself, but in many ways Rome and her territories were now much better governed than they had been for many years. The lives of many people, especially the plebeians (common people) at the bottom of society, were greatly improved.

But it is unlikely that Caesar had the welfare of his people in mind. The only person he really cared about was himself. His position of dictator was the prize he had won after years of careful planning and scheming. However, he did not enjoy his new powers for long.

▲ This pavement mosaic shows a Roman warship carrying soldiers down the River Nile in Egypt. Caesar was fascinated by the great wealth and ancient history of Egypt.

## A new calendar

The old Roman calendar was not very accurate. In 45 BC, Caesar replaced it with a new calendar, now known as the Julian Calendar. It had 365 days in a year, with an extra day each fourth February to keep in line with the seasons. We still use this 'leap year' system today.

# One demand too many

In 44 BC, Julius Caesar seemed untouchable. But the old noble families that he had stripped of their traditional powers were just biding their time. A man with so much power inevitably had many enemies. The moment he slipped, they would pounce.

### Caesar wants to be king

In March 44 BC, Caesar called a meeting of the **Senate** at which, it is claimed, he demanded that he should now be made king. This title would mean that when Caesar died, his adopted son would become the next ruler.

The senators were horrified by this demand. It went against everything that Rome had stood for since the city's first kings had been expelled, more than 400 years earlier. Caesar's lust for power had gone too far – this was one demand too many.

### Murdered in the Senate

A group of senators, led by Marcus Junius Brutus, started plotting against Caesar. On 15 March 44 BC, Caesar went to the Senate to hear the response to his demand. Everyone rose to their feet as he entered the Senate house and walked to his throne at the end of the main chamber.

◀ This bronze Roman coin was made during Julius Caesar's rule as **dictator**. It bears his portrait and the **inscription**, 'Caesar Dictator'.

Then a group of senators, including Brutus, surrounded Caesar as if they were going to ask him questions. One of them suddenly pulled out a dagger and stabbed Caesar in the shoulder. All the others then fell on Caesar like a pack of wolves. He died almost immediately, falling to the ground at the base of the statue of his great rival, Pompey.

▲ This detail of a painting by the 18th-century Italian artist, Vincenzo Camuccini, shows Caesar being stabbed to death by the senators.

### Beware the Ides of March!

A soothsayer (someone who predicts the future) had warned Caesar, 'Beware the *Ides* of March!' The *Ides* was the fifteenth day of that month, and it fell on the day Caesar was to hear the Senate's reply. As he entered the Senate house, Caesar spotted the same soothsayer. Caesar is supposed to have said to the man that the *Ides* of March had come and he was unharmed, to which the soothsayer replied, 'They have come, but they are not yet gone'.

# After Julius Caesar

As soon as news of Caesar's murder spread, street fighting and riots broke out in Rome. The senators abolished the **dictatorship** and tried to restore the old **republican** system of government. Caesar's great-nephew, Octavian (whom Caesar had adopted as his own son at the beginning of 44 BC), and another **politician** called Mark Antony opposed this return to power by the old **patrician** families.

▼ This tapestry, showing Caesar on horseback, was made in Flanders about 1500 years after his death. He was still regarded as one of the most important figures in history.

◀ Caesar adopted Octavian as his son just a few months before he was killed. When Octavian became emperor in 27 BC he was given the title of Augustus, which means 'revered one'.

## Civil war

Octavian and Mark Antony were supported by most of the common people of Rome and also by a large part of the Roman army. **Civil war** broke out between this group on one side and the **Senate** and the rest of the army on the other. In 42 BC the Senate was defeated, but nine years later Octavian and Mark Antony fought against each other in yet another civil war. This time Mark Antony was defeated, and Octavian became the first Roman **emperor**, taking the official name of Augustus. The change from a **republic** to an **empire**, which Julius Caesar had begun, was now complete.

## Caesar's legacy

Julius Caesar is one of the most important figures in history. The changes to the Roman system of government that he introduced remained in place for centuries after his death. His brilliant victories in Gaul led to the Roman conquest of much of northern Europe. This changed Rome from a power based around the Mediterranean into a far greater European power.

In the end, Rome ruled one of the greatest empires the world had ever seen. The Roman language – Latin – and Roman ideas and skills dominated Europe and much of the **Middle East** for more than 500 years. Today, the Roman Empire that Julius Caesar helped to create is still seen as one of the world's greatest **civilizations**.

# Glossary

**ambition** strong desire for success

**astronomy** scientific study of the sun, moon and stars

**bribe** money or goods offered in return for service or favour

**campaign** operation, often military, to achieve a single goal

**citizen** member of a state or nation

**civil war** war fought between groups within the same country

**civilization** human society with political, cultural and legal organization

**consul** most senior Roman government official, in charge of the Senate and the army. Two consuls were elected each year.

**corruption** being involved indishonest practice, such as bribery

**culture** shared ideas, beliefs and values of a people

**depose** remove from office or a position of power

**dictator** man who takes control of the government and the army in times of trouble. He made all the political and military decisions.

**emperor** ruler of an empire. The first Roman emperor was Augustus.

**empire** large area of land ruled over by a single person or government

**gladiator** prisoner, criminal or slave who fought for the public's entertainment

**governor** official who ruled a province of the Roman Empire

**Ides** 15th day of March, May, July and October and the 13th day of each other month

**inscription** words carved into stone or on a coin

**Middle East** area around the eastern Mediteranean Sea, from Turkey to North Africa and eastwards to Iran

**monk** man who is a member of a religious community

**orator** someone who makes a speech in public

**patricians** upper class of Roman citizens, descended from the oldest noble families. In early republican times, only patrician men could become senators.

**philosophy** study of the world, the purpose of the universe and the nature of human life

**piracy** robbery on the seas

**politician** person involved in government

**politics** business of governing and running a country

**praetor** senior judge and the governors of some provinces

**province** area outside Rome, but under Roman control

**ransom** payment of money for the release of a prisoner

**republic** a state governed by people who are elected

**scholar** learned person

**senate** group of officials who governed Rome

**slave** servant who was the property of his or her master

**talent** ancient unit of money

**tribe** group of people, defined in terms of common descent, territory, culture

**tribune** Roman elected by the plebeians to represent them in the Senate

**Triumvirate** joint rule of Rome and her empire by three men: Caesar, Pompey and Crassus

**tutor** teacher hired to teach a child at home

# Timeline

| | |
|---|---|
| 753 BC | Date traditionally given for the founding of Rome. The city is ruled by a series of kings. |
| 510 or 509 BC | Last king expelled from Rome and a republic is formed |
| By 264 BC | Rome becomes the most powerful state in Italy |
| About 100 BC | Birth of Julius Caesar |
| 82–79 BC | Sulla rules as dictator |
| 78 BC | Death of Sulla |
| 70 BC | Marcus Crassus and Gnaeus Pompey are consuls |
| 59 BC | Caesar is made consul |
| 58–50 BC | Caesar's campaigns in Gaul |
| 55–54 BC | Caesar's invasions of Britain |
| 53 BC | Death of Crassus |
| 48 BC | Pompey is killed |
| 46 BC | Caesar is created dictator for life |
| 44 BC | Assassination of Julius Caesar |
| 31 BC | Caesar's great-nephew and heir, Octavian, defeats Antony and Cleopatra at the Battle of Actium |
| 27 BC | Octavian becomes the first Roman emperor, and takes the title of Augustus |

# Further reading & websites

*All in a Days Work: Emperors and Gladiators*, Anita Ganeri, Heinemann Library, 1997
*Legacies From Ancient Rome*, Anita Ganeri, Belitha Press, 1999
*The Roman News*, Andrew Langley, Walker Books, 2000
*These were the Romans*, G. Tingay and J. Badcock, Hulton Educational, 1998
*Heinemann Explore* – an online resource from Heinemann.
For Key Stage 2 history go to *www.heinemannexplore.com*
www.bbc.co.uk/education/romans/home.html
www.romans-inbritain.org.uk

# Places to visit

Roman Baths at Bath                    Hadrian's Wall in Northumberland
Museum of London, London.

# Index

Alexander the Great
13
Antonius Gnipho    7
Apollonius Molon    10
Aurelia    6

Britain    19
Brutus, Marcus Junius    26

Calpurnia    17
Calpurnius Piso    17
Cinna    8
Cicero, Marcus Tullius    20
citizens    9
Cleopatra    23
consuls    17, 18, 20
Cornelia    8, 13
corona civica    10
Cossutia    8
Crassus, Marcus Licinius    14, 17, 20
Curule Aedile    14, 15

death of Julius Caesar    4, 26–7
dictator    24, 26

early life    6–7

family    6

Gaul    18, 19
gladiators    14, 15
Greece    23

Ides of March    27

Julia    8, 17, 21
Julian calendar    25

Mark Antony    23, 28, 29
marriage    8, 13, 17
Minucius Thermus    10

Octavian    28, 29

patricians    7, 9, 28
Pharmacusa    10
Pharsalus    23
pirates    10–11
plebeians    25
Pompeia    13
Pompey    13, 16, 22
    as consul    20
    death of    23
    marriages    17, 21
Pontifex Maximus    15
praetor    6, 16
Ptolemy XIII    23

Quaestor    12

Rhodes    10, 11
River Rubicon    22
Roman Empire    5, 29
Rome    4

Scipio, Metellus    21
schooldays    7
Senate    9, 16, 24, 26, 29
senators    20
slaves    6, 22
Sulla, Lucius Cornelius    9

tribune    12
Triumvirate    16, 17, 20

Vercingetorix    19

# Titles in the Life and World of series include:

Hardback      0 431 14765 5

Hardback      0 431 14771 X

Hardback      0 431 14774 4

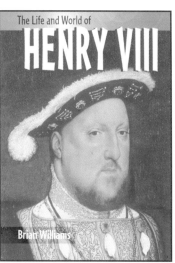

Hardback      0 431 14767 1

Hardback      0 431 14775 2

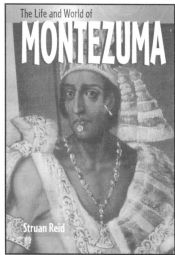

Hardback      0 431 14763 9

Hardback      0 431 14769 8

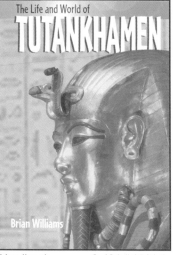

Hardback      0 431 14761 2

Find out about the other titles in this series on our website www.heinemann.co.uk/library